The New Quilt 1

Dairy Barn Quilt National

The Taunton Press

Front cover: detail of *Keep Both Feet on the Floor*
by Yvonne Porcella (the full piece is shown on
page 1). Back cover: detail of *Utage* by Sachiko
Yoshida (the full piece is shown on page 53).
Photographs: Susan Kahn.

© 1991 by The Taunton Press, Inc.
All rights reserved.

First printing: June 1991
Printed in the United States of America

A THREADS Book

Threads® is a trademark of The Taunton Press, Inc.,
registered in the U.S. Patent and Trademark Office.

The Taunton Press, 63 South Main Street, Box 5506,
Newtown, CT 06470-5506

Library of Congress Cataloging-in-Publication Data

The New quilt 1 : Dairy Barn Quilt National.
    p.   cm.
    "A THREADS book" — T.p. verso.
    Exhibition catalog of Quilt National '91, the seventh in a series of biennial
international competitions held by Dairy Barn Southeastern Ohio Cultural Arts
Center.
    Includes index.
    ISBN 0-942391-99-3
    1. Quilts — History — 20th century — Exhibitions.   I. Dairy Barn Southeastern
Ohio Cultural Arts Center.   II. Title: Dairy Barn Quilt National.
NK9110.N4   1991   91-9238
746.9'7'0904807477197 — dc20   CIP

Acknowledgments

The Dairy Barn Southeastern Ohio Cultural Arts Center takes pride and pleasure in presenting Quilt National '91, the seventh in the series of biennial international competitions for contemporary art quilts. By providing a showcase for the work of talented fiber artists from throughout the world, we hope to encourage people to recognize quiltmaking as a vital art form that will be increasingly important in the twenty-first century.

We would like to acknowledge the efforts and support of all those who contributed to the success of the project. We are particularly grateful to jurors Tafi Brown, Esther Parkhurst and Rebecca A.T. Stevens for their patience and obvious commitment to the responsibility they accepted; to The Taunton Press for their cooperation and concern for the quality of this publication; to the Quilt National '91 sponsors: the Ohio Arts Council, the Ohio Department of Development Office of Travel & Tourism, the Fairfield Processing Corporation (maker of Poly-fil® brand fiber products) and the City of Athens; and to the countless volunteers from the Athens community who contributed their time and support for this event. We would also like to thank the hundreds of artists who shared their work with us. Their innovative expressions continue to delight and amaze. To all, we offer our most sincere appreciation.

—*Lynn Buckingham,*
Executive Director
—*Hilary Morrow Fletcher,*
Quilt National Coordinator

Introduction

When The Dairy Barn Southeastern Ohio Cultural Arts Center organized the first of its biennial Quilt National exhibits in 1979, the purpose was "to promote the contemporary quilt as an art form." Since then, hundreds of thousands of people have experienced the best of the world's art quilts through Quilt National, its catalogs and touring exhibits. For quilt artists, Quilt National remains the pinnacle, and both the number of artists submitting entries and the number of works submitted have increased by more than 300% from Quilt National '79 to Quilt National '91.

Quilt National '91 drew 1,178 entries from 594 artists in 14 nations. New countries added to the list in 1991 include Finland, New Zealand, the Republic of South Africa and Yugoslavia. Japan and Germany continue to head the list of foreign countries with the largest number of entries.

The jurying process resulted in an exhibit of 76 works by 69 artists from 26 states and four other nations. In their statement (see pages 81-82), the jurors describe the contemporary quilt as an art form characterized by a period of "consolidation" and "maturity of style." Their observation is reinforced by the artists' statements in this catalog.

Over and over, the artists reflect confidence, pride and joy in what they do. No apologies, no explanations are needed. The once worrisome issue, "Is it art or craft?," has become a question that amuses more than perplexes the contemporary quilt artist. Art, yes, but art growing out of and enriched by a specific tradition. Several artists speak of the moment when they realized that, as Chris Wolf Edmonds puts it, a "lifelong avocation could be a stimulating vocation" or, as Libby Lehman says, "a profession and a passion."

More and more of the artists are working in a series, shaping and reshaping idea and image. More are creating their own materials —dyeing, painting and stenciling fabric; using photo processes; embellishing and combining fabrics—to create the palette they need. All have been "seduced by fabric," in Ellen Oppenheimer's words.

The contemporary quilt remains predominantly a woman's art form, one Quilt National Coordinator Hilary Fletcher says, "perhaps always will be, given women's social history and affinity for the needle arts." Most of the artists have formal training and degrees in painting, sculpture, graphic design or fiber arts, but they have grown up watching other women sew and been initiated into the tactile and visual pleasure of working with fabric. Many express satisfaction that comes from combining traditional woman's handwork with fine art and drawing on the idioms of traditional quiltmaking.

Since the first Quilt National, many other exhibits of art quilts have been organized, more museums and galleries are exhibiting contemporary quilts, and more and more artists are having works commissioned by corporations and individuals. Looking back over more than a decade of promoting the contemporary quilt, The Dairy Barn takes pride in its leading role in putting forth the contemporary quilt as an art form, and looks forward with confidence to organizing future exhibits as quilt artists the world over continue their explorations.

Traveling Show's Itinerary

After the opening exhibition of Quilt National '91 at The Dairy Barn in Athens, Ohio, the show travels to several other sites during the next two years. At press time, the itinerary was just beginning to take shape, and the bookings below had been confirmed. For information about the show's complete itinerary, call The Dairy Barn Cultural Arts Center at (614) 592-4981.

St. Louis, Missouri
The Gallery at St. Louis Center
Nov. 18 to Dec. 31, 1991
(Show sponsored by The Women's Self-Help Center)

Pueblo, Colorado
Sangre de Cristo Arts Center
April 16 to May 28, 1993

Yvonne Porcella
Modesto, Calif.

*Keep Both Feet
on the Floor*
Cotton fabrics.
Machine pieced,
hand appliquéd,
hand quilted; hand-
embellished and
hand-painted
backing fabric.
54 in. by 77 in.

This title of this piece was inspired by a trolley ride at Dollywood in Pigeon Forge, Tennessee. After picking up the tourists in the parking lot, the trolley tour guide announced that the trolley would not proceed toward the entry gate until everyone had "both feet on the floor and all body parts inside..." One year ago I tore the

cartilage in my right knee while getting up from the sewing machine. I had three months of physical therapy. All the patients were busy doing some form of exercise on legs, arms, shoulders, elbows and knees. This quilt is about falling first and then building up muscles through exercise.

Risë Nagin
Pittsburgh, Pa.

Exile: House and Mountain
Various fabrics including silks and cottons, some of which are stained and painted. Hand pieced, hand appliquéd and hand quilted. 82 in. by 54 in.

"Exile: House and Mountain" is part of an ongoing series of works that take as their subject issues concerning domesticity, shelter, security, loss of innocence, betrayal, and patterns of power in relationships between men and women and children.

AWARD FOR BEST OF SHOW

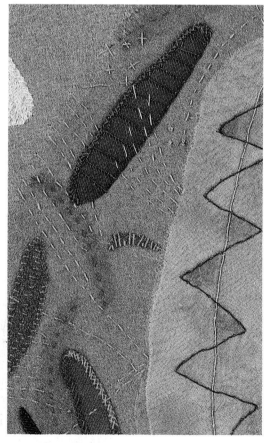

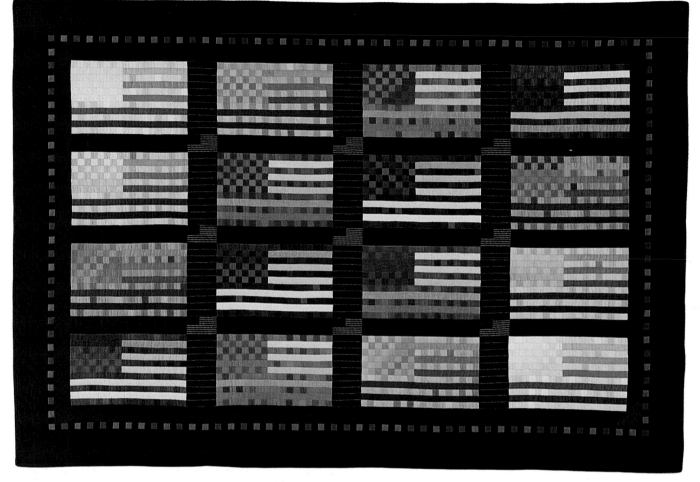

Carol H. Gersen
Boonsboro, Md.

Squares and Bars
Commercial and
hand-dyed fabrics.
Machine pieced,
quilted by hand
and machine.
77 in. by 52 in.

Inspiration for this quilt came from the 1988
Presidential election campaign, moving to a
house with a flagpole and to a state with a
wonderful flag, 4,000 tiny squares remaining
from a previous project, and the use of our
flag in American folk art.

**DOMINI McCARTHY MEMORIAL
AWARD FOR EXCEPTIONAL
CRAFTSMANSHIP**

Pamela Studstill
Pipe Creek, Tex.

Quilt #91
Cotton fabrics.
Machine pieced and
hand embellished
with textile paint;
hand quilted by
Bettie Studstill.
74 in. by 74 in.

This quilt is an attempt to capture the
diversity and monotony of existence
through repetition and variation.

AWARD OF EXCELLENCE

Michael James
Somerset Village,
Mass.

Crosscurrent 3
Cotton and silk
fabrics. Machine
pieced, machine
quilted. From a
private collection.
43 in. by 43 in.

"Crosscurrent 3" is one of a recent series of quilts that deals with water and the movement of water, especially the unseen undercurrents beneath the surface that are, for me, metaphors for the emotional undercurrents that flow through our lives.

Helen Giddens
Dallas, Tex.

Wash Day Whirls
Cottons and blends.
Machine pieced,
machine quilted.
87 in. by 67 in.

All my quilts are made of "scraps," and
these fabrics are washed before I piece them.
This particular quilt represents one of those
days when I've been blessed with someone's
grandmother's cousin's aunt's scrap bag.
When I prewash the fabric it looks
something like this in the machine. Each
piece is a different size, shape and print.
There is only one print repeated. I think of
this as a contemporary charm quilt.

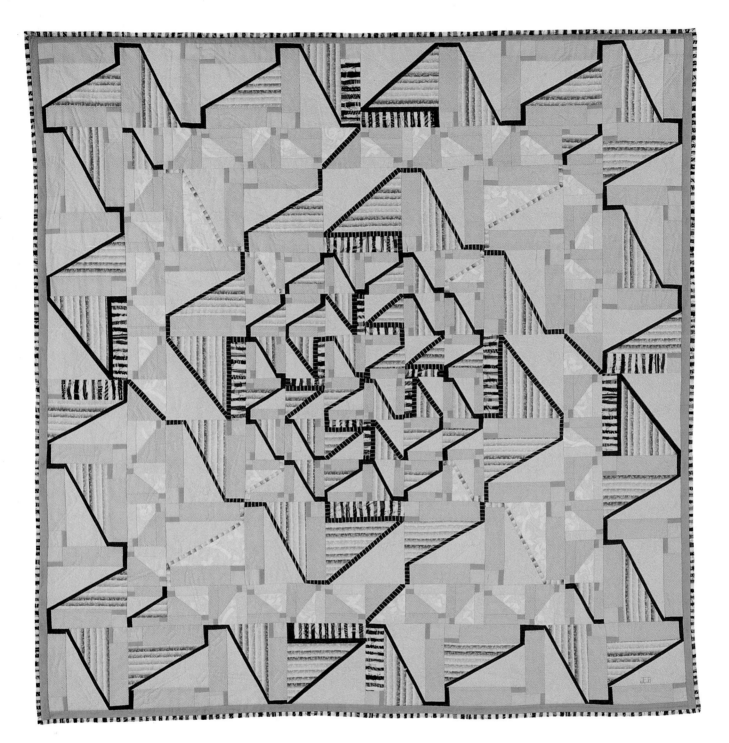

Judy Becker
Newton, Mass.

Response to Granada
Cotton fabrics.
Machine pieced
and hand quilted.
64 in. by 64 in.

Spain and the Moors are names that evoke a sense of mystery and exoticism. This quilt is a response to a trip to Granada to see the fantastic architecture of the Alhambra Palace. The background reflects the sun-bleached plains leading to the hills of Granada. The surface design is my personal synthesis of the lavishly embellished facades of the Alhambra.

Roxana Bartlett
Boulder, Colo.

*Darkness Was About
To Pass*
Various fabrics, dyes,
paints and inks.
Surface design
applied by hand,
appliquéd and
quilted by hand.
57 in. by 57 in.

My quilts are filled with images of
landscape and animals that are symbolic of
the untamed external natural world and of
the untamed world of our inner selves.
These images are like the feelings that enter
through the senses. They move through our
hearts and minds as those in dreams — more
clearly felt than seen and understood.

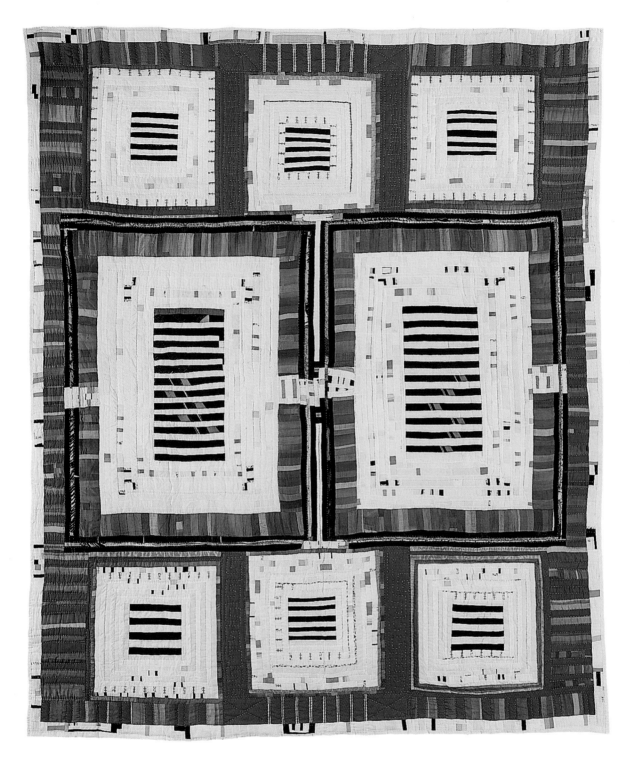

Elizabeth Vohler
Berlin, Germany

STR 1
Commercial and
hand-dyed fabrics
including cotton,
silk and wool.
Machine pieced
and hand quilted.
77 in. by 84 in.

The old "log cabin" is still in my head. The
old and perfect design. But let it turn into
our weird presence, so that the simple
blocks will fall apart and even lose their
square shapes. Stability vanishes, and what
comes through is a glimmering nervousness.

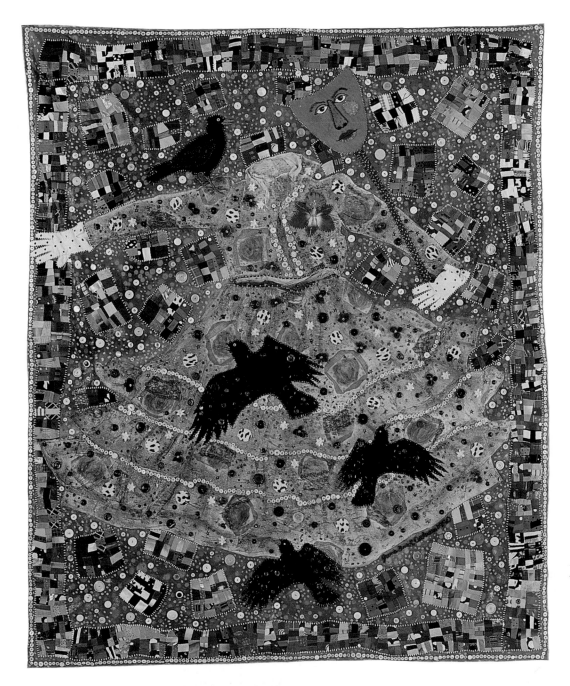

Jane Burch Cochran
Rabbit Hash, Ky.

The Last Dance
Assorted fabrics,
buttons, beads, paint
and found objects.
Machine pieced and
appliquéd by hand,
hand embellished.
69 in. by 79 in.

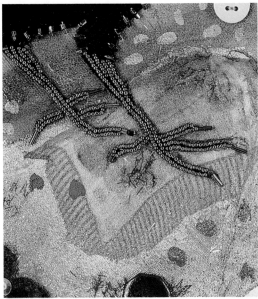

This quilt was conceived when I found an
old dress made of cheesecloth in a bag of
rags. I attached the dress to the canvas
background using a thin coat of gesso.
I painted and embellished the dress and
added the gloves, mask and blackbirds. The
quilt seems to tell a story, but the narrative
developed on its own and is for the viewer
to determine. The batting and backing are
attached by the buttons, using the tie
method. In this quilt the patchwork is part
of the background, which is a different
approach for me.

Ellen Oppenheimer
Oakland, Calif.

Flinderation
Cottons and blends.
Machine pieced,
hand and machine
quilted. 101 in.
by 71 in.

This quilt is about the Loma Prieta
earthquake in October, 1989. I had
envisioned that a serious earthquake in
downtown San Francisco would rain broken
glass from all the tall buildings. I had
imagined that anyone walking in the streets
would be cut into so many little pieces by
these clear glass flinders [fragments] falling
from the sky. In this respect the earthquake
was more benign than I expected. This quilt
is what I had imagined it would be like.

Patty Hawkins
Lyons, Colo.

*Beyond the Blue
Horizon*
Commercial and
hand-dyed cottons
and blends. Machine
strip-pieced, machine
quilted. 79 in.
by 79 in.

The illusion of space is created by light
shafts emanating from an unknown source
beyond the foreground grid of arrow
shapes, which can be read as space vehicles.
While we are all busy exploring our
universe, we also need to protect our planet,
searching for ways to reduce pollution.
With any artistic statement also comes
a responsibility.

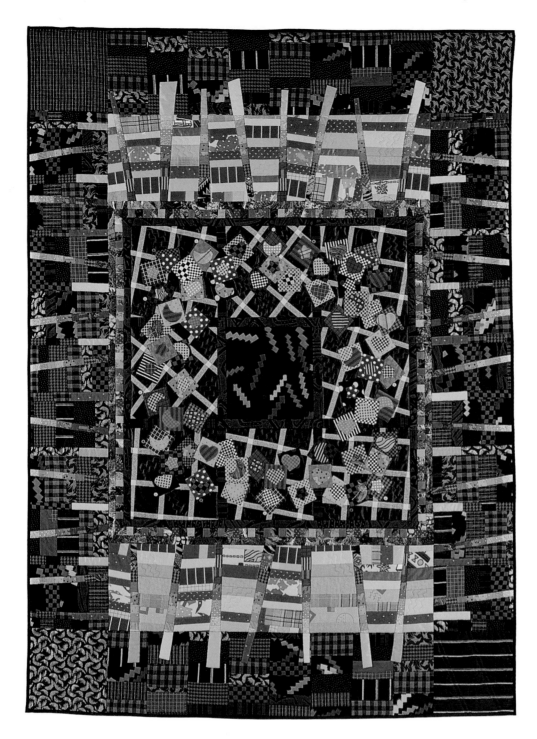

Faye Anderson
Denver, Colo.

*Basheer's Surprising
Dinner Cruise*
Commercial and silk-
screened cotton
fabrics. Machine
pieced, hand
appliquéd and
hand quilted.
41 in. by 80 in.

Of many memorable events on my 1989 trip
to India, the most spectacular and exotic
was a dinner party with a Kashmiri family
on a rustic boat on Dal Lake at the city of
Srinagar. The color, motion and energy of
the music and dance seemed to reverberate
in shock waves out into the black water and
night sky. This is the mood I have tried to
recreate in my quilt.

Erika Carter
Bellevue, Wash.

Dedication
Cottons and blends.
Machine pieced,
hand appliquéd and
hand quilted. From a
private collection.
50 in. by 63 in.

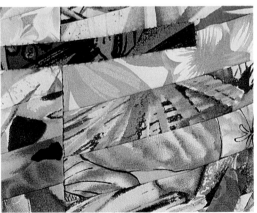

This work was inspired by a view from my window. The wild dogwoods portray winter dormancy's patient wait for spring.

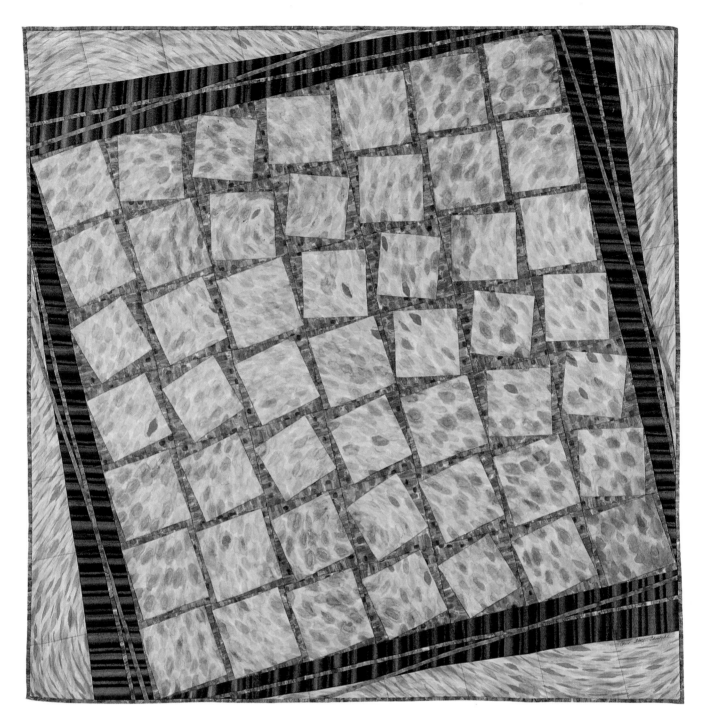

Chris Wolf Edmonds
Lawrence, Kan.

Spin #2
Hand-painted cotton
fabric. Machine
pieced and quilted.
50 in. by 50 in.

The "Spin" series is an outgrowth of a year of commission work for U.S. Sprint. Seventeen rectangular pieces based on a system of sequentially rotated squares have been created for their offices across the country. The relatively simple design concept and construction allow for endless variation in the hand-painted color of the fabrics. The interplay between the color patterns and the values in the series of twisted squares within squares helps to create an illusion of motion in the designs. Color and pattern for the fabric in this work were inspired by the paintings of Monet and Van Gogh.

Linda Ruth MacDonald
Willits, Calif.

Search for Pattern
Cotton print fabric.
Airbrushed, painted
and hand quilted.
84 in. by 81 in.

One of my interests is the study of textiles
from around the world. In this piece,
through airbrush and paint, I am alluding to
the interlacing of fiber materials and to
varied construction techniques. During the
painting, chance occurrences and newly
discovered avenues led me into new arenas.

Lisa Beaman
Austin, Tex.

Head Series I:
Shattered
Cotton fabrics.
Machine pieced,
hand appliquéd
and hand quilted.
41 in. by 41 in.

This quilt is the first in a series that explores inner emotions and states of a psychological nature. "Shattered" depicts the moment when we discover our world isn't as it appears—through growth and exploration it disintegrates into a new reality.

Susan Shie
and
James Acord
Wooster, Ohio

The Earth Quilt; a Green Quilt
Leather, crocheted fabric, paint, buttons, beads and other found objects. Hand worked and stitched. 83 in. by 91 in.

Some blessings and healing energy for the Earth are sewn and painted into this quilt, the first in a four-part series for the basic natural elements: earth, water, air and fire. Its four-legged animal totems represent earth energy, and its many spirit masks and dolls celebrate the daily ritual of caring for our planet and each other. The quilt commemorates the 20th anniversary of the May 4th incident at Kent State University, during which four students were killed. The work is dedicated to our grandma Elvira Acord, who died at age 82 while this work was in progress.

L. Carlene Raper
Putney, Vt.

North Woods
Hand-dyed cotton
fabrics. Machine
pieced, backed and
tied. 48 in. by 61 in.

"North Woods" is the result of a
combination of planning and serendipity.
Working on a huge trestle table outdoors,
I hand-dyed a piece of cloth many colors,
blending them into each other. I had the idea
of zigzag piecing, and after figuring out how
to produce the effect, I went ahead and did
it, ending with nine strips of more or less

random color placement. I then arranged
these as they are now. In a sense, I let the
piece make itself; I let chance make some of
the decisions that I as an artist might
ordinarily make. Then again, I've made the
choice to let chance make them!

Linda Levin
Wayland, Mass.

Barcelona: Gaudí I
Procion-dyed
cottons. Machine
pieced, machine
quilted. 69 in.
by 56 in.

This is the first in a series (three so far)
based on the buildings in Barcelona that
were designed by the great architect
Antonio Gaudí. This one was inspired by
a wonderful park he designed in which the
man-made forms imitate nature.

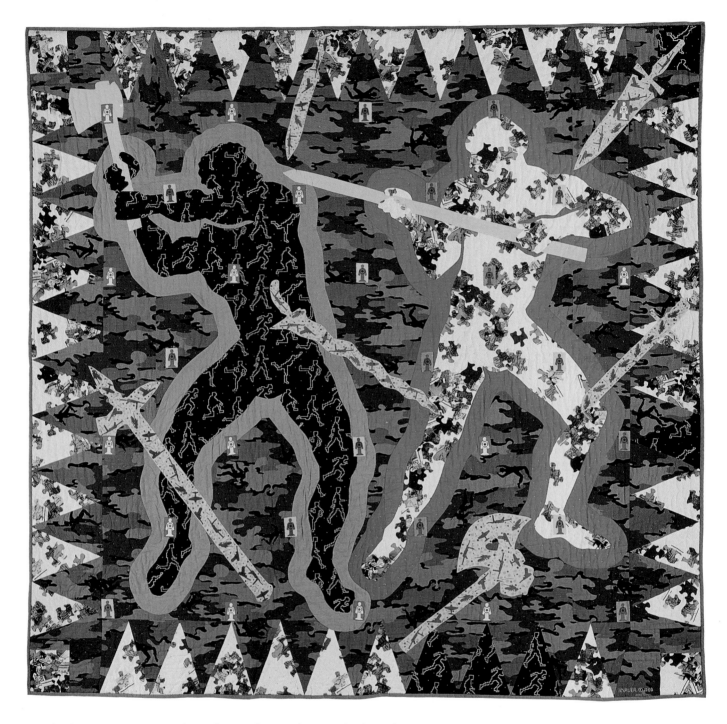

Katherine Knauer
New York, N. Y.

Conflict
Various fabrics.
Machine pieced,
stenciled, hand
appliquéd and hand
quilted. 88 in.
by 85 in.

When I began this work, I was looking for an opportunity to use two wonderful printed fabrics together. The original intent was to depict a type of generic, universal combat: men versus women, humanity versus technology. The result, however, was overwhelmingly racial in theme. This work was completed during the time the Howard Beach case was a daily feature of television news and, sadly, the beginning of a recent wave of racial violence.

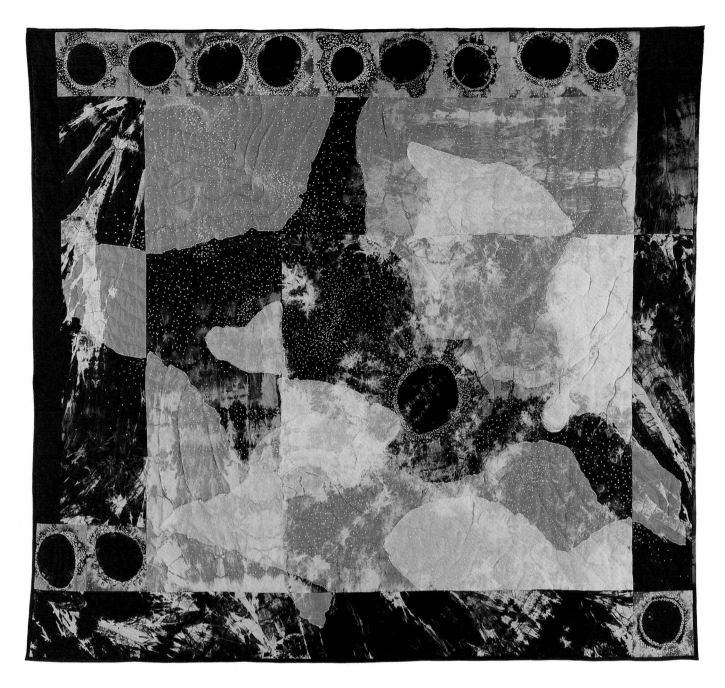

Nancy Crasco
Arlington, Mass.

...of black holes and the ozone layer
Discharge-dyed black cotton painted with silver metallic marker. Machine pieced and hand quilted. 62 in. by 57 in.

Recently a friend who is an astronomer told me that within one year we will have a photograph of a black hole. Unless we reduce our carbon-dioxide emissions and the use of fluorocarbons to save our protective layer of ozone, we will not be able to appreciate the wonders of the heavens.

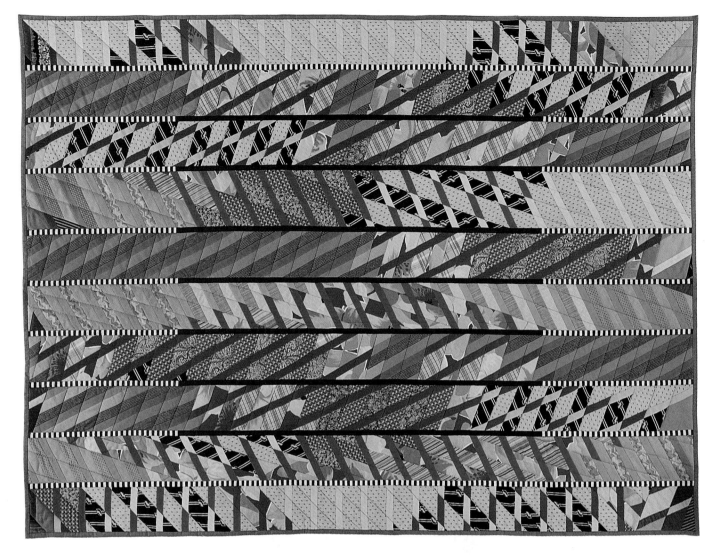

Esther Parkhurst
Los Angeles, Calif.

Reconstructed Hot Rhythms
Cottons and blends. Machine pieced, machine and hand quilted. 68 in. by 51 in.

This was an experiment to see if I could duplicate something that happened by chance at a previous time. I developed a large strip-pieced quilt so that I could recut it into large strips and then reorganize all·of it and create a somewhat fractured result. I like the result, and I will continue to experiment with this notion.

INVITATIONAL: Quilt National '91 Juror

Deborah J. Felix
San Diego, Calif.

*Old American
Proverb: Time Scars*
Various fabrics,
vinyl and paint.
Direct and reverse
appliquéd, hand
quilted by Susan
Plack. 53 in. by 93 in.

This piece was created to record a difficult time in my life. At that time people often gave me words of wisdom, such as "time heals, the future will be brighter..." and so on. I decided that there ought to be an American proverb that would say that time scars but never truly heals, it just covers over our wounds. Fortunately, time has healed this piece for me.

Kathi Casey
Southlake, Tex.

Mesa Sky
Hand-painted cotton sateens, cotton, velvet and satin. Machine pieced, quilted by machine and by hand. 65 in. by 63 in.

This is part of a series about the sky—I love to gaze into the sky and become lost in it. On one of my frequent visits to New Mexico, I was overwhelmed by the sky there—it is unlike the sky anywhere else in the world.

Sally Sellers
Vancouver, Wash.

The Tines, They Are A-Changin'
Commercial cottons and blends. Machine pieced, machine quilted. 84 in. by 68 in.

"The Tines, They Are A-Changin'" is my second quilt exploring the wonderful design of the everyday fork. I have always been intrigued by ambiguous boundaries and the process of transition. Few things are certain—I attempt to befriend this idea in my work so as not to be frightened by it.

Nancy Erickson
Missoula, Mont.

Night of the Golden Stars
Hand-painted cottons and satins. Machine appliquéd and machine quilted. 108 in. by 57 in.

The sky is very black, the stars and constellations brilliant as I walk to the mailbox to pick up the paper on early winter mornings. This work is part of a series celebrating twilight. The lions, somewhere in time, are just passing through—as are we all.

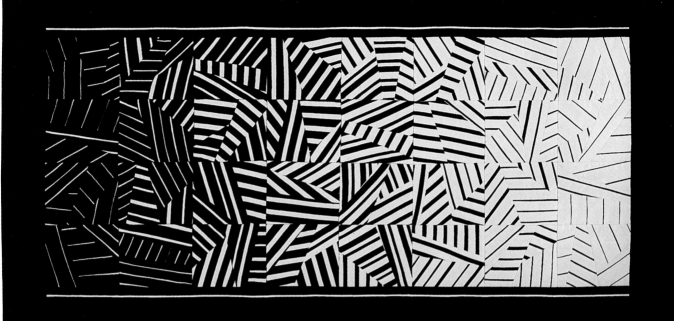

Sally Knight
Burlington, Vt.

Still Crazy
Cotton fabrics.
Machine pieced,
machine quilted.
40 in. by 20 in.

I began this piece as a personal challenge to see what effect I could get using only black and white. As I worked, I kept thinking how, in contrast to my youth, almost nothing seemed just black and white anymore, but instead a complex, ever-changing blend of the two. I'd always hoped things would get easier—or at least clearer—as I got older. I should have known better. It's still crazy!

Joan Schulze
Sunnyvale, Calif.

Perennial Border
Cottons and silks.
Machine appliquéd,
embroidered and
quilted, hand painted
and hand appliquéd.
81 in. by 62 in.

"Perennial Border" is a reflection on
gardens, especially after a rain.

Anneke Herrold
Greencastle, Ind.

Backyard View
Cottons and blends.
Machine sewn to
backing pieces.
63 in. by 80 in.

This is part of a series of quilts in which I
have surrounded "crazy quilt" squares with
a fence-like lattice. The bottom squares are
darker to resemble shady ground, while the
top opens to lighter sky-like space. Real and
illusory layers interest me.

Jane Burch Cochran
Rabbit Hash, Ky.

Fan Flirts
Assorted fabrics,
buttons, beads, paint
and found objects.
Patchwork, machine
strip-pieced and
appliquéd by hand.
43 in. by 60 in.

The inspiration for this quilt is obviously the
fan quilt pattern. I beaded the eyes and
appliquéd the gloves to make the "flirt"
blocks. I added the unrelated block to keep
the quilt from being too predictable.

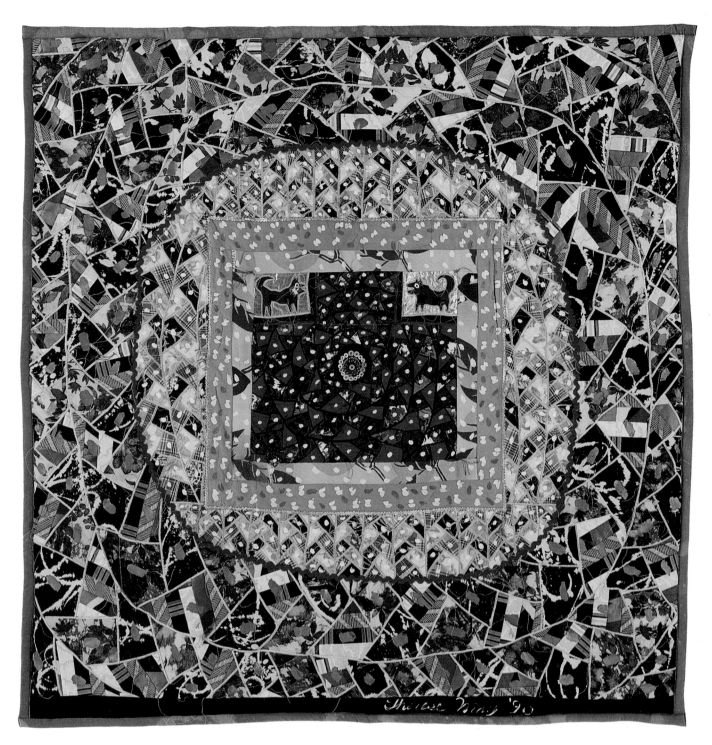

Therese May
San Jose, Calif.

Abundance
Cotton fabric, acrylic paint, rickrack trim and buttons. Machine appliquéd and quilted; hand embroidered. 65 in. by 65 in.

"Abundance" —an affirmation of world peace and my fervent hope that there will be enough to go around.

Elizabeth A. Busch
Stonington, Maine

Last Picture Show
Acrylic paint on raw
cotton canvas treated
with colored pencils
and procion dyes;
commercial fabric,
embroidery floss.
Hand brushed
and airbrushed;
machine pieced;
hand appliquéd,
embroidered
and quilted.
89 in. by 67 in.

We are all involved with landscape every
day, both external and internal, looking out
and looking in. Sometimes there is a balance
of importance; sometimes one facet
outweighs the other, and the lesser view
becomes peripheral.

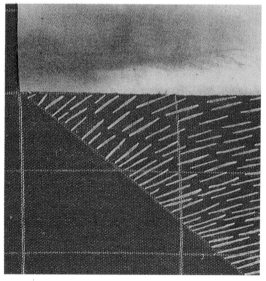

Beth Thomas Kennedy
Austin, Tex.

A Nuestra Señora La Virgen de Guadalupe
Cottons, blends and oilcloth. Machine pieced and quilted; hand appliquéd and hand embellished with beads, milagros and other religious and ethnic objects. 77 in. by 76 in.

I am fascinated by the limitless scope of working with fabric. The work I do awakens an intuitive sense of color, texture and light. Although nontraditional in nature, my quilts draw on the idioms of traditional quiltmaking, adding new dimensions that generate new forms and new ways of representing what I see. This work is part of a series that celebrates matriarchal rituals, expressing the impact of women on culture and society.

Lori J. Barks
Carbondale, Ill.

*Through Grandfather's
Eyes: Lori and Drew
at Thanksgiving*
Cyanotype on cloth.
Hand painted and
machine quilted.
27 in. by 20 in.

My interest in the historical family image
began when I was given a box of my
grandfather's slides. The amount of
information that was forgotten—the faces
that I hadn't remembered in detail, the
places that no longer existed—were frozen,
preserved as they once existed, in
Kodachrome. I was intrigued by the fact that
if these slides didn't exist, these places and
times that were once so important to me
would have been forgotten forever. The
family dinner is preserved in these quilts to
be passed down as quilts are traditionally
passed down within a family. Since I wanted

my images to represent a more universal
family rather than my specific family, I hid
the identities of the figures. The image
stresses the importance of the family dinner,
and sees it today as a fleeting moment in a
time when relationships are so complicated.
Family dinners of the past were like quilts,
with the same planning, preparation and
community involved in their making.
Family dinners today are like horse
blankets—a quick buy and a poor
substitute, with hardly the love and the joy
that goes into the making of a quilt.

Miriam Nathan-Roberts
Berkeley, Calif.

Tectonic Boogie
Cotton fabrics.
Machine pieced,
appliquéd and
quilted. 65 in.
by 69 in.

On October 17, 1989, at 5:04 p.m., the San Francisco area was rocked by a major earthquake. In the months that followed we experienced many aftershocks—real and imaginary. I seemed to live in a state of "hyper-reality." When I started this quilt, I worked spontaneously—the only limit I put on myself was not to make an earthquake quilt because I thought a lot of people in this area would be making

them. When I finished the quilt I realized that I had, indeed, made an earthquake quilt. The movement of tectonic plates causes earthquakes.

Ellen Oppenheimer
Oakland, Calif.

Kishkas
Cottons and blends.
Machine pieced,
machine quilted.
80 in. by 82 in.

Kishkas is a Yiddish word that translates literally as "intestines." Because there is a 100-ft. long, convoluted and continuous line that travels through this quilt, this seemed an appropriate name. The title also suggests that my most sensitive insides, my guts, are in some manner infused in this quilt.

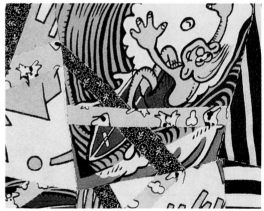

Fran Skiles
Plantation, Fla.

Stepping Out of Line
Hand-painted
cottons and silks.
Machine pieced and
quilted with metallic
and nylon thread.
49 in. by 39 in.

This quilt is an outpouring of spontaneity,
a fabric graffiti. The message is a joy for the
technique of placing paint on fabric and
discovering the combinations.

Barbara J. Mortenson
Melrose Park, Pa.

Tied Woman
Cottons and blends.
Machine pieced
and quilted; hand
appliquéd on reverse
side. 40 in. by 40 in.

I love the shapes a figure makes. They never lose their fascination for me. This shape was inspired by a long-loved photo. Why is she tied?...Why do we let ourselves get tied down, tied up?

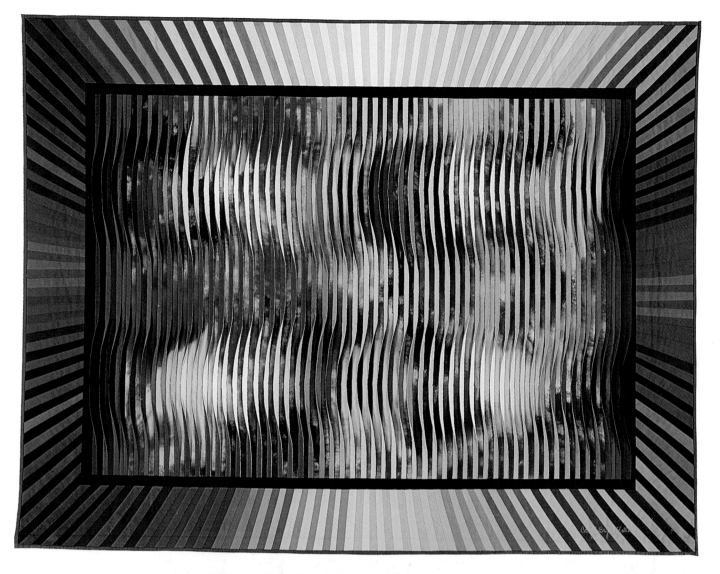

Caryl Bryer Fallert
Oswego, Ill.

High Tech Tucks #21
Hand-painted and
hand-dyed cotton
fabric. Machine
pieced, machine
quilted. 65 in.
by 49 in.

This is one of a series of quilts in which
three-dimensional constructed tucks are
incorporated into a patterned background.
The background fabric is painted with dyes
and then cut into strips. The tucks are
constructed with one side being a value
gradation from black to white, and the other
side being a gradation of pure rainbow
colors. The tucks are then inserted into
the seams of the reassembled background.
The machine quilting twists the tucks to
one side or the other to create the illusion of
movement and light across the surface
of the quilt.

Judith Vierow
Columbus, Ohio

"Net" - Egyptian
AllMother
Printed and batiked
cotton fabrics,
buttons. Machine
and hand stitched.
56 in. by 92 in.

In ancient Egypt, "Net" is the source of all
creation, the original mother from whose
menstrual blood the entire universe, all
the gods and goddesses were created.

She is the result of my own search for the
black goddess and has touched a deep
creative source within.

Françoise Barnes
Colorado Springs,
Colo.

Mask for a Visionary
Cottons and blends,
some of which are
hand dyed. Machine
pieced by the artist
and hand quilted by
Mrs. Lewis Yoder.
72 in. by 72 in.

This is the fifth and final mask in the Zaïre
Series. The look is almost weightless and
ethereal. It gave the maker/wearer
inescapable, clear vision…

Judith H. Perry
Winnetka, Ill.

About Jazz
Cotton fabrics.
Machine pieced,
machine quilted.
47 in. by 47 in.

"About Jazz" is the first in a series that explores my experience with jazz —music that speaks to my mind, my heart and soul. Jazz absorbs the influences that surround it, interweaving the textures and richness of different cultures into something unique and wonderful. It makes order out of chaos and transforms the ordinary into the remarkable. Jazz is about improvisation and spontaneity —about taking risks and breaking the rules —about drinking it all in, the full existence, the very rhythm of life.

Linda Levin
Wayland, Mass.

Pallone: Papaveri
Procion-dyed
cottons. Machine
pieced, machine
quilted. 35 in.
by 52 in.

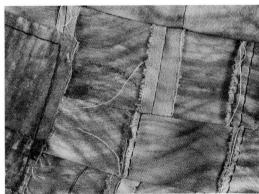

This quilt is part of a series based on hot-air balloon trips over Siena, Italy. *Papaveri* is Italian for "poppies," and this piece is an aerial view of the poppy fields, which were blooming at the time.

Katherine Knauer
New York, N. Y.

Flying Cadet, 1943
Various fabrics and
found objects. Hand
stenciled, hand
embellished,
embroidered by hand
and by machine.
67 in. by 67 in.

The subject of the portrait at the center of
the work is my father-in-law, Conrad
Knauer, as he looked during World War II.
The cartoon-like motifs throughout the piece
are typical "nose art" — squadron insignia
painted on the front end of military aircraft.
The work is intended to add to the dialog on
"art versus craft" by using a combination of
quiltmaking and painting techniques, which
make it difficult to categorize.

Jean Neblett
San Francisco, Calif.

Primal III
Commercial and
hand-dyed fabrics
made by Eric and
Nina Morti of Katy,
Tex. Machine pieced
and machine quilted
with cotton, rayon
and metallic threads.
61 in. by 47 in.

The central shape, itself suggesting
movement, is surrounded by a turbulence
reminiscent of an undersea waving
landscape, constantly slightly disturbed…
the turmoil of growth.

Ann Brauer
Charlemont, Mass.

even in January there is
the promise of spring
Silk fabrics. Machine
pieced onto muslin
facing. 55 in. by 45 in.

I am fascinated by doors and what lies
beyond the entrance — possibilities, hope.
Each of my works is a statement of a feeling.
In this work I was exploring the fact that
even when life is the darkest, there is always
the knowledge that another door will open
and out of the dark, new life will flow.

Marquerite Malwitz
Brookfield, Conn.

Desert Sunrise: Desert Botanical Garden, Phoenix, AZ
Cotton, blends, linen and silk; hand dyed, painted and beaded. Machine pieced; hand and machine quilted; hand embroidered, appliquéd and beaded. 41 in. by 52 in.

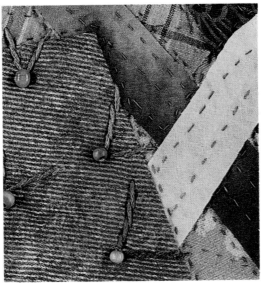

Cactus forms and desert settings continue to challenge my creativity and design direction. Although a trip to the Desert Botanical Garden in Phoenix initially inspired this quilt, a further jolt of inspiration came from a trip to Santa Fe, where I observed an art community that is not afraid to use color. A biblical verse that I have assigned to this work is Isaiah 51:3: "And her wilderness He will make like Eden, and her desert like the garden of the Lord."

Wendy C. Huhn
Dexter, Ore.

Trick-or-Treat
Cotton and blended
fabrics, some treated
to glow under black
light or in the dark.
Machine pieced,
hand quilted and
embellished with
shrink-art skull
charms. 30 in.
by 22 in.

I won't grow up! I love holidays—this quilt
is my way of celebrating Halloween.

Elizabeth A. Busch
Stonington, Maine

Focus
Acrylic paint on raw
cotton canvas treated
with colored pencils;
commercial fabric,
embroidery floss.
Hand brushed and
airbrushed; machine
pieced; hand appliquéd,
embroidered and
quilted. 67 in. by 68 in.

Spatial and geometric illusions with an
unfamiliar palette were my concerns in this
work. This was the last of eight pieces I did
at the Leighton Artist Colony in Banff,
Alberta, Canada. I intentionally used colors
not in the range of the other works in order
to jar me out of a "safe" color mode.

Kathleen O'Connor
Putney, Vt.

Spike
Hand-dyed cotton
fabrics. Machine
pieced and quilted.
53 in. by 77 in.

I want my pieces to say, "I am," in a clear, personal and often assertive way. I'm after the kind of effect that a childhood smell has when reencountered: a feeling immediate, familiar and whole yet resonant and mysterious. Many of the fabrics are hand dyed because I enjoy both the control and the surprises hand dyeing affords me. I love the feeling that, within the quilt's borders, I can make anything happen.

Sachiko Yoshida
Saitama, Japan

Utage
Silk fabrics. Crazy
patchwork. 79 in.
by 79 in.

This quilt was made to show the excitement
of a party and also the let-down that occurs
after the guests have gone. The light colors
represent the joy and laughter of being with
friends. The dark portions represent the
loneliness that comes after the party.

Nancy Erickson
Missoula, Mont.

Restless Mountain
Hand-painted
cottons, satins and
velvets. Machine
appliquéd and
machine quilted.
103 in. by 94 in.

All of my work of the last seven years is
about the humor and tenacity involved in
communities of individuals during times of
chaos, disintegration and fragmentation.
The capybaras, ravens and lions are
acknowledged powerful elements in life.
They act as familiars or spiritual guides. In
this piece the mountain, too, is speaking.

Janet Page-Kessler
New York, N. Y.

After the Fall
Artist's canvas,
cottons and blends,
paint. Machine
appliquéd,
embroidered and
quilted; hand
painted. 42 in.
by 30 in.

This piece is about devastation and also
about optimism, hope and faith. As with
most natural, man-made or personal
catastrophes, after the fall, ultimately,
strange and newly wonderful things or
circumstances begin to develop—which
the symbolic imagery of this piece
reflects. Possibly it will invoke the viewer's
own interpretation.

I would like to acknowledge the
involvement of my daughter, Susan Kessler
Neill, in this quilt. Although she did not
physically assist in the construction, her
creative input and support pushed me past
a creative block encountered midway
through this piece and led to its completion.

Jan Myers-Newbury
Pittsburgh, Pa.

Hot Spot
Cotton fabric hand
dyed and tie dyed
with procion dyes.
Machine pieced and
quilted. 72 in.
by 74 in.

This entire piece was designed in relation to
the green tie-dyed fabric. This is the first
time I've left large unpieced sections in a
quilt, and the first time I've used undyed
(white) fabric. The graphic boldness of
"Hot Spot" is a departure for me, perhaps
an arrival!

Keiko Gouke
Miyagi, Japan

Summer Time in Vermont
Cotton fabrics. Machine pieced; hand appliquéd and quilted. 71 in. by 83 in.

I traveled to Vermont in July, 1990. Lake Champlain shone brightly. The brightly colored wildflowers were in full bloom everywhere.

Holley Junker
Sacramento, Calif.

From A Darkened Window
Coin-sized, pinked circles of commercial and hand-dyed cotton fabric and Mylar chiffon. Layered and machine stitched to base fabric and hand quilted. 37 in. by 34 in.

This quilt is part of a recent series of "nightscapes"—views of distant landscapes as lit by a night sky.

Tafi Brown
Alstead, N. H.

B.W. and Company on Pratt Road
Cyanotype prints on commercial and hand-dyed fabrics. Machine pieced, hand and machine appliquéd, machine quilted. 56 in. by 76 in.

This is a personal story quilt about the dirt road on which I have just had my house built. There have been many timber-frame raisings on my road. This quilt is about the joy that all my neighbors and friends take in building houses and helping others. It is about the timber-framing company for which I used to work. It is about the men and women who work there and for whom the company has helped to build their homes. It is about the trees and flowers that bloom in the spring...my associations with and on Pratt Road.

INVITATIONAL: Quilt National '91 Juror

Sharon Heidingsfelder
Little Rock, Ark.

Serving Millions From Atop the Alleghenies
Hand-dyed and commercial cottons. Machine pieced by the artist, hand quilted by Graffie Jackson. 86 in. by 66 in.

When finished, this quilt reminded me of the Allegheny Mountains in Johnstown, Pa., where I grew up. The title is (was) the slogan of the local television station, "Channel 6, WJAC, Serving Millions from Atop the Alleghenies."

Darcy Usilton
Madison, Wis.

Because it is Bitter and Because it is My Heart
Various fabrics including wool, velvet and satin. Machine pieced and quilted, hand embellished with yarns and threads. 72 in. by 55 in.

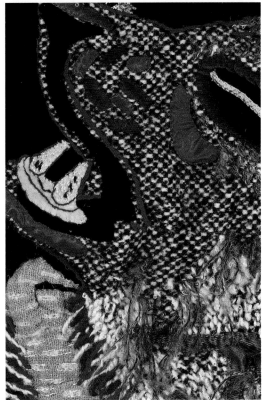

Three years ago my husband had a heart transplant. A year and a half later, he left me. Having already completed a series of work on the transplant, I wanted to end the three years by creating a work for me. The wolves in this piece are my protectors—easing me through my "bitter heart" time.

Jane A. Sassaman
Chicago, Ill.

Heaven's Gift
Commercial cottons
and blends. Machine
pieced and appliquéd;
machine quilted.
78 in. by 60 in.

"Heaven's Gift" is about our obligation to
use our given talents. I believe we are given
special abilities to advance our civilization
and the evolution of our souls. By
embracing our talents, we not only fulfill
our purpose on earth but also glorify the
Giver. This quilt symbolizes the joyous
exchange of gifts between heaven and earth.

Robin Schwalb
Brooklyn, N. Y.

Babel
Photo-silkscreened, stenciled, painted and commercial fabrics. Machine pieced, and hand appliquéd and quilted by Karen Berkenfield, Margit Echols, Susan Ball Faeder, Katherine Knauer, Leslie Levison, Diane Rode Schneck and Robin Schwalb. 89 in. by 72 in.

The biblical story of the tower of Babel explains that the proliferation of languages is a result of a sort of divine pre-emptive strike against an uppity mankind. Here a modern skyscraper undergoing demolition is a perfect stand-in for the biblical tower, but it also serves as a metaphor for my life during the past year. Within a six-week period of 1989, I traveled to Japan, returned to New York, bought and moved into a new home and severely injured my wrist. (Thanks, dear friends, for helping me quilt this thing!) Not being sufficiently stressed out by all of the above, I decided to try to learn Japanese—a move that made me question my intelligence, sanity and the possibility of communication between people, anywhere, ever!

Dee Ann Todd Teague
Sugarland, Tex.

Rainforest
Cottons and blended fabrics. Machine pieced, machine quilted. 67 in. by 67 in.

The clearing of the rainforests is symbolic of humankind's destruction of the environment. The frog is disappearing. Although camouflaged by strip piecing, fragmentation and exploded images forebode extinction.

Libby Lehman
Houston, Tex.

Frenzy
Commercial cottons
and hand-dyed
cottons by Eric and
Nina Morti. Machine
pieced, appliquéd
and quilted. 76 in.
by 86 in.

This piece was created organically, with each
step leading to the next. No templates,
drawings or patterns were used. It is the
first of a series on emotions. I had planned
to start with "solitude" but, as is obvious,
that is not the direction my life is taking!

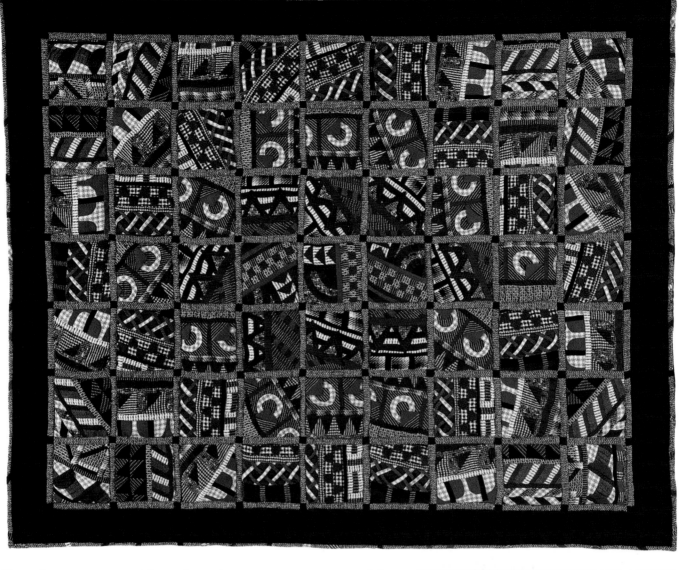

Karen Larsen
Cambridge, Mass.

Wool Crazy 6 - Colors on a Rainy Day
Wool fabrics. Machine and hand pieced and appliquéd; plaiting, pleating and other techniques used to produce various raised surface textures. 90 in. by 73 in.

The quilts in this series are my version of the traditional Victorian crazy quilt. Most of the pieces in the series are based on a single abstract block, which is repeated and rotated to give the impression of both movement and balance. Blocks of the later pieces, like this one, are based on enhanced strip-piecing techniques. I work in wool because I find that the depth of the colors, the textures and the weaves are irresistible, and unmatched in any other fabric. The pleating and various other surface textures remind me of the work I used to do as a theatrical costume designer.

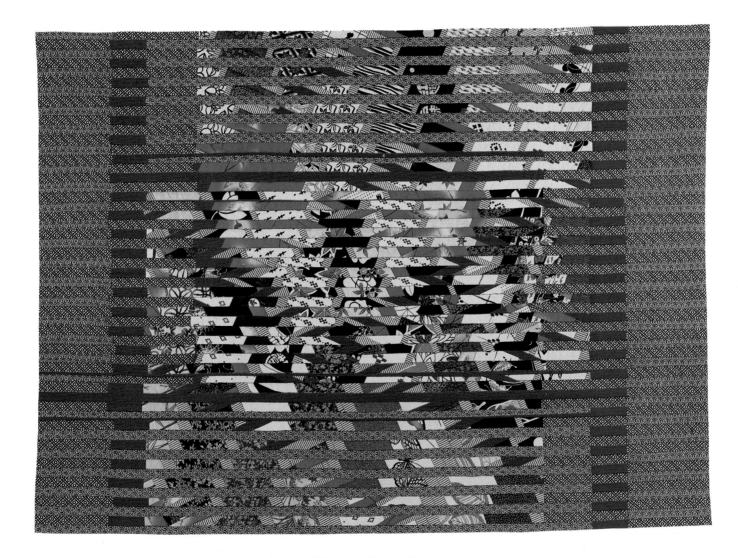

Nancy Gipple
Afton, Minn.

Kinji Akagawa's 50th Birthday Quilt
Domestic and imported cottons. Machine pieced and quilted. 105 in. by 75 in.

My spouse was born in Tokyo and spent his first 22 years there. He is proud to be a first-generation American, with two wonderful children here. At the same time he deeply misses his family and country of birth. This quilt includes some Japanese fabrics that were given to me by his family. This quilt is my attempt to bring two places together for him, at once.

Jan Myers-Newbury
Pittsburgh, Pa.

Precipice
Cotton fabric hand
dyed and tie dyed
with procion dyes.
Machine pieced and
quilted. 75 in.
by 93 in.

"Precipice" began as a formal response to a
piece of tie-dyed fabric that ultimately was
not used Along the way the quilt
accompanied me on a spiritual journey,
and it became a visualization of that
journey. The simplicity of its form belies the
struggle in fact.

Natasha Kempers-Cullen
Bowdoinham, Maine

On a Clear Day You Can See Forever
Cotton broadcloth, fiber-reactive dyes, metallic threads, glass beads. Hand painted, hand and machine quilted, hand embroidered and embellished. 42 in. by 66 in.

This is the first work in a series based on song titles and is a manifestation of hope and a positive attitude. The piece was inspired by my work at Spindleworks, a sheltered workshop for mentally handicapped adults, who are eager to engage in creative activity. There were pots of geraniums on the windowsills and colorful paintings, drawings and handwoven items everywhere. I began this piece there in the workroom and came to realize that if only we can get beyond ourselves, we can see that beauty and clarity do shine through turmoil and misfortune.

Janet L. Patek
Cameron, Mo.

High School Graduation
Cottons and blends. Machine pieced and appliquéd. 65 in. by 42 in.

Having an active, eclectic personal life in addition to my role as a mother, I never thought that I would have time to be affected by the empty-nest syndrome. However, as two of my teenagers reached the age of departure, "High School Graduation" came to me with an impact that forced me to reevaluate the rhythms of my life and my being. This work, one of a series on raising teenagers, chronicles my exit from the known.

Nancy Taylor
Pleasanton, Calif.

My Road to California
Cottons and blends.
Machine pieced and
hand appliquéd;
hand quilted by
Margaret Vautine.
76 in. by 100 in.

My husband and I grew up in the Midwest
and wanted to move to California. However,
school and job changes took us first to
Arizona and Texas, then Louisiana, and
finally, eight years later, to California. The
road in the center foreground reflects that
journey. The bright colors at the top seem
appropriate to depict the liveliness and
diversity of our destination.

Katie Pasquini-Masopust
Oxnard, Calif.

Dimensional Portal
Cottons, blends and lamé fabrics.
Machine pieced, reverse appliquéd and hand quilted.
83 in. by 83 in.

The idea for this quilt came from a suggestion from my husband to do a piece with round poles that turn and interlock. Many months later, this is what happened. I tried to get the feeling that you could climb around inside this structure with its different levels.

Betty E. Ives
Windsor, Ontario, Canada

Pieces of Time
Various fabrics and dyes. Machine pieced; hand appliquéd, quilted, embroidered and embellished. 68 in. by 56 in.

This quilt was created especially for the 1990 Threads of Friendship Contest in Odense, Denmark, at which it received a Special Judges Commendation Award. I thoroughly enjoy using various types of fabrics and those that I have collected from my world travels. The title "Pieces of Time" has a double meaning: time to collect, design and crate, and the many "time" spans in the various fabrics used—from apes to the 1980s designs and the button clocks.

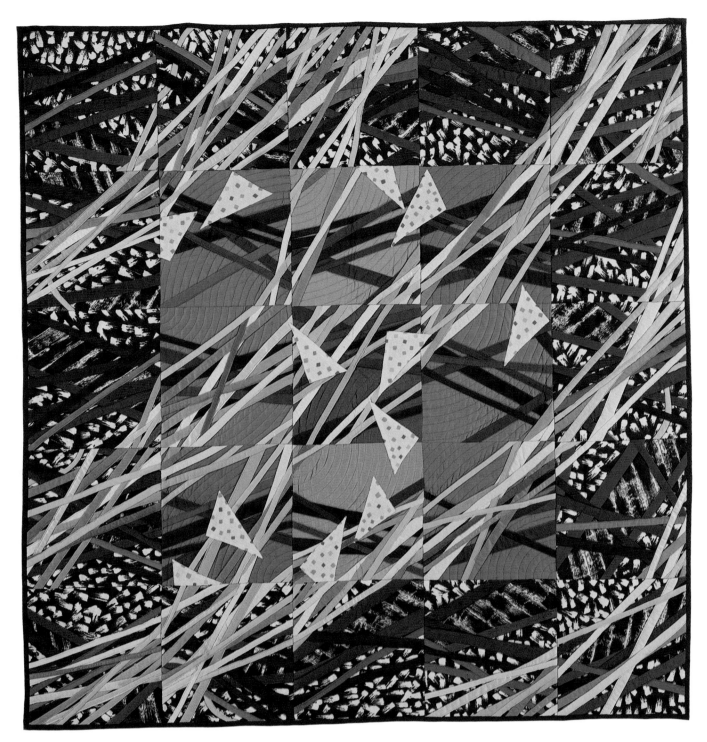

Sue Alvarez
Fries, Va.

Spring Snows
Cotton fabrics.
Machine pieced and
quilted, appliquéd by
hand and machine.
43 in. by 43 in.

Making the intuitive quilt frees my spirit.
This quilt was stitched during the last
snowstorm of spring. Remembering these
days gives me pleasure, which I hope, here,
to share with the viewer.

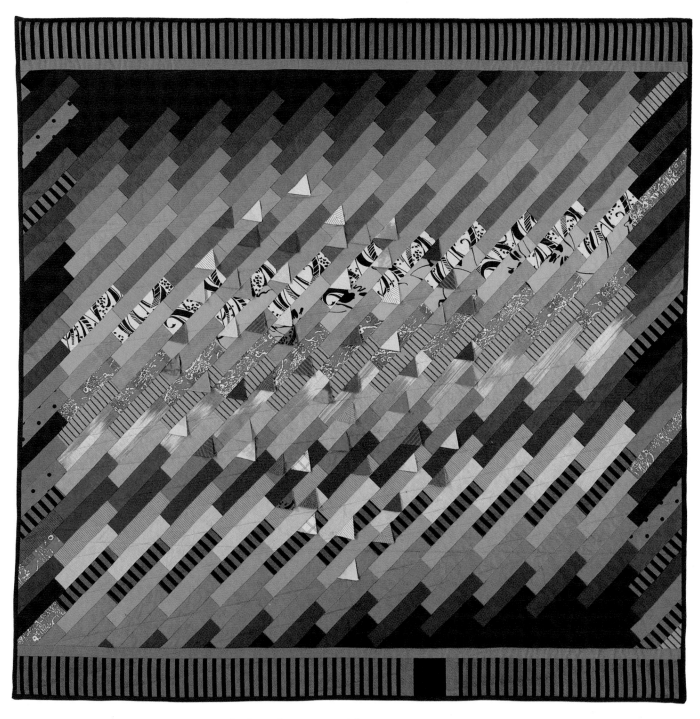

Mary Morgan
Little Rock, Ark.

Silver Bells and Cockle Shells
Hand-dyed and commercial cottons, some of which are overdyed. Machine pieced and quilted. 46 in. by 44 in.

I have never had much success raising flowers. This is my fantasy garden where everything is lush and vibrant and where petals fall at random. And, yes, sometimes I am quite contrary…

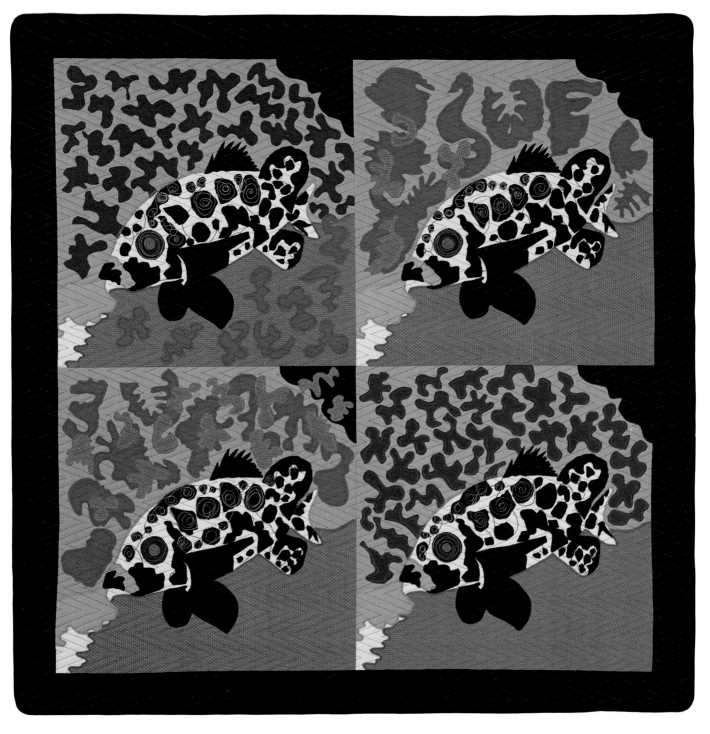

Pauline Burbidge
Nottingham,
England

Sweetlips
Cotton fabrics.
Machine pieced and
appliquéd, quilted
with an industrial
quilting machine.
36 in. by 36 in.

This quilt marks the beginning of a series
based on fish images. I was particularly
attracted to this "clown sweetlips" fish
as it rested in front of a coral, creating
a camouflage with its spotted body.

Erma Martin Yost
Jersey City, N. J.

Spirit Pass
Canvas designed
with paint, pastels,
markers and
cyanotype images.
Machine pieced,
embroidered and
quilted. 38 in.
by 32 in.

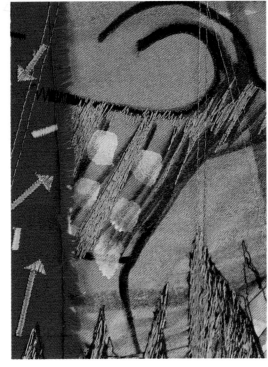

I hand-paint or print the fabrics I use. The printing processes are photographic, and to create the image I use Kodalith negatives. For the hand-painted fabric, I use acrylic and metallic paints and iridescent pigments. All of these fabrics are cut up and machine embroidered before reassembly. The imagery, landscape and vast sky refer to the American Southwest, where I have spent considerable time over the last 15 years seeking out ancient Indian rock paintings on canyon walls. At these sites there exists a strong sense of place and importance. These are places that have been frequented by generations, places of ritual and ceremony. I try to capture the essence of these places in my work.

About the Jurors

Robert H. Brown

Tafi Brown's academic background is in art education, art history and ceramics. She was the recipient of a Fulbright/Hayes Grant to study in Belgium and The Netherlands. Students at all levels from elementary to college have had the benefit of her teaching. Her work has allowed her to combine her interest in fiber art with her interest in photography. By using the process of cyanotype (developing blueprints on fabric), she has been able to incorporate images of trees, buildings and people into the design of her quilts. Brown's quilts have been seen in dozens of exhibits and publications. She is also represented in numerous corporate collections such as IBM, Georgia Power Corporation, Holiday Inn Restaurant Services and the Fulbright Alumni Association. Much of her recent work reflects yet another interest — building timber-frame houses, including her own recently completed home. When she is not involved with the visual arts, Brown participates with the Marlboro Morris and Sword Dance Team, which, through its performances, maintains the traditions of ritualistic Anglo-Saxon folk dancing.

Ken Parkhurst

Esther Parkhurst is a native Californian who studied at the University of Southern California and Chouinard Art Institute in Los Angeles. She began her abstract fabric constructions in 1979 and has gained national and international recognition. Numerous corporate spaces throughout the country have her work on display, including the Hilton, Hyatt-Regency, Marriott and Sheraton hotels; The Hallmark Corporation; Columbia Pictures; Verdugo Hills Hospital and the Plum Tree Restaurant. Parkhurst has taught and lectured at several nationally known museums and academic institutions. Her quilts have been shown in group and solo exhibits from Massachusetts to California and have also been featured in *Fortune* magazine as well as the major fiber-arts publications.

Andrea V. Uravitch

Rebecca A.T. Stevens has an extensive academic background at universities and art schools in the United States and England. Her experience as a teacher, lecturer, juror, art consultant and craftsperson have provided her with a broad-based knowledge of issues and ideas in contemporary arts and crafts. Numerous scholarly publications have featured her articles on crafts in general and fiber art in particular. Institutions with which she has had professional involvement include the Renwick Gallery, National Museum of American Art, Smithsonian Institution; James Madison University, Harrisonburg, Va.; and the Arlington (Va.) Art Center. Stevens currently works as a private art consultant for various organizations and individuals and serves as the Consultant for Contemporary Textiles at The Textile Museum in Washington, D. C.

Jurors' Statement

urying Quilt National was an exciting, exhausting and rewarding experience—exciting because it provided the opportunity to see over 1,100 new works from all over the world; exhausting because it took time to make thoughtful decisions; rewarding because it resulted in an exhibit and catalog that document an important event in the quilt world. Implicit in the charge to the jurors was the responsibility both to the artists who submitted their work and to the thousands of visitors who will see the show on its two-year tour to select a group of works that, when seen together, represent the best of current, contemporary quiltmaking—"the state of the art." The job was made pleasant and efficient by the exhibit's talented coordinator, Hilary Fletcher, and her team of dedicated quilt-loving volunteers. They were able to answer all of our questions and meet our every request in the course of the judging. Without them, our job would have been impossible.

The jurying process began on a Friday evening, when we had a first look at all the entries, and ended two days later, after more than sixteen hours of reviewing the slides and discussing the merits of the quilts these slides presented. As with any selection made entirely from slides, the quality of the photographs was a factor in our decisions. If we couldn't see the quilt clearly, we couldn't include it in the exhibit. When each piece appeared on the screen, we all asked ourselves: Is the piece well designed? Well executed? Is it an original artistic statement, or is it a "knock-off" of a previously exhibited piece?

Each juror had her own criteria. We are different, and those differences strengthened our collective judgment as we discussed which pieces would be included and why. Ms. Stevens looked for works that pushed the boundaries of quiltmaking and demonstrated a strong personal voice. Ms. Brown looked for pieces that spoke to her visual intellect as well as her emotions, pieces that proclaimed their presence in an unself-conscious way. Ms. Parkhurst responded to works that presented a strong graphic image, and also exhibited original, unique, innovative methods and statements. We considered each work at least twice before making any decisions about its inclusion in the show.

We think Quilt National '91 documents a turning point in the history of the contemporary quilt. It signals a period of consolidation, a new maturity of style. Gone are the self-conscious attempts to startle the viewer, proclaiming the maker's independence from historical precedents. On the contrary, those precedents are embraced. The artists whose work is represented in this exhibition have produced quilts very much in the mainstream of the quiltmakers who have gone before them. There is a dialog with historical antecedents: album quilts, crazy quilts, pattern quilts. There was a decided preference for surface design techniques (photo transfers) and surface embellishment, a continuance of the tradition found in nonfunctional 19th-century quilts. There is a return to the rectilinear plane, with an emphasis on strong color and design. There is less experimentation and a clear desire to work within the quilt vernacular. This year an award for the most innovative use of the medium seemed inappropriate because

no single work represented a new departure or new phase in the quiltmaker's vocabulary. Instead of technical novelties, we found impressive craftsmanship and technical prowess in the 76 works in this exhibition. Quiltmakers are comfortable with their own genre and do not feel the need to reach into other art spheres. This exhibition is an affirmation, a joyous celebration of quilts as art.

What does the future hold for contemporary quilts? Only the next Quilt National and contemporary quiltmakers can tell.

—*Tafi Brown*
—*Esther Parkhurst*
—*Rebecca A. T. Stevens*

About the Dairy Barn

he Dairy Barn was built in 1914 as a farm structure. Constructed on land belonging to the Athens Mental Health Center, it originally housed nearly 200 animals, which were tended by patients as part of the farm therapy program. It was home to Lotta Faye Korndyke, the 1929 World Champion cow that produced more than twice the milk of the average cow. With strides in mental health therapy and the emphasis on de-institutionalization, the patient population at the center decreased; by 1968, it was only one-tenth what it had been at the turn of the century. Part of the dairy farm complex had been destroyed by fire, and the remaining structure stood idle.

In 1977, only nine days before the scheduled demolition of the barn, area resident and artist Harriet Anderson and her husband Ora led a community effort to save the building. Working with members of the Hocking Valley Arts Council, the Andersons established The Dairy Barn Southeastern Ohio Cultural Arts Center, a nonprofit corporation. In 1978 the facility was also placed on the National Register of Historic Places and thereby spared from the threat of future demolition.

During its first decade, The Dairy Barn was transformed from a makeshift exhibition space to a first-rate art gallery with climate

A view of Quilt National '89.

control, security systems, lighting and display apparatus, and a neutral, but not stark, environment in which to showcase art. Today the twelve-month program calendar includes juried international exhibits, festivals and programs of regional interest, as well as performances and activities that appeal to visitors of all ages.

The Dairy Barn is supported by admissions, memberships, corporate sponsorships and various grants. The staff is assisted by the invaluable efforts of volunteers who work tirelessly to see that "their" Dairy Barn is able to provide the kind of programming that has come to be expected.

The purpose of the Dairy Barn is to promote the arts, crafts and cultural heritage of southeastern Ohio by serving as a showcase for the best of what is available in the region. Through the many exhibits of new or historic work of national and international importance, The Dairy Barn also provides residents of the area with opportunities to experience the arts and culture of individuals from whom they are separated by miles or generations. The Dairy Barn Southeastern Ohio Cultural Arts Center's proximity to Ohio University and its reputation in the international art community make it a highlight on the itinerary of visitors from all over the world.

Index

Editor: Hilary Morrow Fletcher
Designer: Deborah Fillion
Layout Artist: Christine Timmons
Photographer: Susan Kahn, except as noted
Copy/Production Editor: Ruth Dobsevage

Typeface: Palatino
Paper: Warrenflo, 80 lb., neutral pH
Printer: Ringier America, New Berlin, Wis.